Murder in the Cathedral

MURDER
in the
CATHEDRAL

BY T. S. ELIOT

A Harvest Book
HARCOURT, BRACE & WORLD, INC.
New York

Murder in the Cathedral

THIS play was written for production (in an abbreviated form) at the Canterbury Festival, June 1935. For help in its construction I am much indebted to Mr. E. Martin Browne, the producer, and to Mr. Rupert Doone; and for incidental criticisms, to Mr. F. V. Morley, and Mr. John Hayward.

April 1935

In the second edition a chorus was substituted for the introits which, in the first edition, constituted the opening of Part II. To this third edition the introits have been added as an appendix, and may be used instead of that chorus in productions of the play.

At the suggestion of Mr. E. Martin Browne, I have in Part II reassigned most of the lines formerly attributed to the Fourth Knight. When, as was originally intended, the parts of the Tempters are doubled with those of the Knights, the advantage of these alterations should be obvious.

June 1937

In this fourth edition certain further rearrangements and deletions have been made, which have been found advisable by experiment in the course of production.

March 1938   T. S. E.

Part I

*

Characters

A Chorus of Women of Canterbury
Three Priests of the Cathedral
A Messenger
Archibishop Thomas Becket
Four Tempters
Attendants

*The Scene is the Archbishop's Hall,
on December 2nd, 1170*

CHORUS

Here let us stand, close by the cathedral. Here let us
   wait.
Are we drawn by danger? Is it the knowledge of safety,
   that draws our feet
Towards the cathedral? What danger can be
For us, the poor, the poor women of Canterbury? What
   tribulation
With which we are not already familiar? There is no
   danger
For us, and there is no safety in the cathedral. Some
   presage of an act
Which our eyes are compelled to witness, has forced
   our feet
Towards the cathedral. We are forced to bear witness.

Since golden October declined into sombre November
And the apples were gathered and stored, and the land
   became brown sharp points of death in a waste of
   water and mud,
The New Year waits, breathes, waits, whispers in darkness.

11

While the labourer kicks off a muddy boot and stretches
his hand to the fire,
The New Year waits, destiny waits for the coming.
Who has stretched out his hand to the fire and remem-
bered the Saints at All Hallows,
Remembered the martyrs and saints who wait? And
who shall
Stretch out his hand to the fire, and deny his master?
Who shall be warm
By the fire, and deny his master?

Seven years and the summer is over,
Seven years since the Archbishop left us,
He who was always kind to his people.
But it would not be well if he should return.
King rules or barons rule;
We have suffered various oppression,
But mostly we are left to our own devices,
And we are content if we are left alone.
We try to keep our households in order;
The merchant, shy and cautious, tries to compile a
little fortune,
And the labourer bends to his piece of earth, earth-
colour, his own colour,
Preferring to pass unobserved.
Now I fear disturbance of the quiet seasons:
Winter shall come bringing death from the sea,
Ruinous spring shall beat at our doors,
Root and shoot shall eat our eyes and our ears,
Disastrous summer burn up the beds of our streams

And the poor shall wait for another decaying October.
Why should the summer bring consolation
For autumn fires and winter fogs?
What shall we do in the heat of summer
But wait in barren orchards for another October?
Some malady is coming upon us. We wait, we wait,
And the saints and martyrs wait, for those who shall be
    martyrs and saints.
Destiny waits in the hand of God, shaping the still un-
    shapen:
I have seen these things in a shaft of sunlight.
Destiny waits in the hand of God, not in the hands of
    statesmen
Who do, some well, some ill, planning and guessing,
Having their aims which turn in their hands in the
    pattern of time.
Come, happy December, who shall observe you, who
    shall preserve you?
Shall the Son of Man be born again in the litter of
    scorn?
For us, the poor, there is no action,
But only to wait and to witness.
[*Enter* PRIESTS.]

FIRST PRIEST
Seven years and the summer is over.
Seven years since the Archbishop left us.

SECOND PRIEST
What does the Archbishop do, and our Sovereign Lord
    the Pope

With the stubborn King and the French King
In ceaseless intrigue, combinations,
In conference, meetings accepted, meetings refused,
Meetings unended or endless
At one place or another in France?

THIRD PRIEST

I see nothing quite conclusive in the art of temporal
  government,
But violence, duplicity and frequent malversation.
King rules or barons rule:
The strong man strongly and the weak man by caprice.
They have but one law, to seize the power and keep it,
And the steadfast can manipulate the greed and lust of
  others,
The feeble is devoured by his own.

FIRST PRIEST

Shall these things not end
Until the poor at the gate
Have forgotten their friend, their Father in God, have
  forgotten
That they had a friend?
[*Enter* MESSENGER.]

MESSENGER

Servants of God, and watchers of the temple,
I am here to inform you, without circumlocution:
The Archbishop is in England, and is close outside
  the city.
I was sent before in haste

14

To give you notice of his coming, as much as was
    possible,
That you may prepare to meet him.

FIRST PRIEST

What, is the exile ended, is our Lord Archbishop
Reunited with the King? What reconciliation
Of two proud men?

THIRD PRIEST

                What peace can be found
To grow between the hammer and the anvil?

SECOND PRIEST

                              Tell us,
Are the old disputes at an end, is the wall of pride cast
    down
That divided them? Is it peace or war?

FIRST PRIEST

                          Does he come
In full assurance, or only secure
In the power of Rome, the spiritual rule,
The assurance of right, and the love of the people?

MESSENGER

You are right to express a certain incredulity.
He comes in pride and sorrow, affirming all his claims,
Assured, beyond doubt, of the devotion of the people,
Who receive him with scenes of frenzied enthusiasm,
Lining the road and throwing down their capes,

Strewing the way with leaves and late flowers of the
season.
The streets of the city will be packed to suffocation,
And I think that his horse will be deprived of its tail,
A single hair of which becomes a precious relic.
He is at one with the Pope, and with the King of
France,
Who indeed would have liked to detain him in his
kingdom:
But as for our King, that is another matter.

FIRST PRIEST
But again, is it war or peace?

MESSENGER
Peace, but not the kiss of peace.
A patched up affair, if you ask my opinion.
And if you ask me, I think the Lord Archbishop
Is not the man to cherish any illusions,
Or yet to diminish the least of his pretensions.
If you ask my opinion, I think that this peace
Is nothing like an end, or like a beginning.
It is common knowledge that when the Archbishop
Parted from the King, he said to the King,
My Lord, he said, I leave you as a man
Whom in this life I shall not see again.
I have this, I assure you, on the highest authority;
There are several opinions as to what he meant,
But no one considers it a happy prognostic.

[*Exit.*]

16

FIRST PRIEST

I fear for the Archbishop, I fear for the Church,
I know that the pride bred of sudden prosperity
Was but confirmed by bitter adversity.
I saw him as Chancellor, flattered by the King,
Liked or feared by courtiers, in their overbearing
    fashion,
Despised and despising, always isolated,
Never one among them, always insecure;
His pride always feeding upon his own virtues,
Pride drawing sustenance from impartiality,
Pride drawing sustenance from generosity,
Loathing power given by temporal devolution,
Wishing subjection to God alone.
Had the King been greater, or had he been weaker
Things had perhaps been different for Thomas.

SECOND PRIEST

Yet our lord is returned. Our lord has come back to
    his own again.
We have had enough of waiting, from December to
    dismal December.
The Archbishop shall be at our head, dispelling dismay
    and doubt.
He will tell us what we are to do, he will give us our
    orders, instruct us.
Our Lord is at one with the Pope, and also the King
    of France.
We can lean on a rock, we can feel a firm foothold

17

Against the perpetual wash of tides of balance of forces
of barons and landholders.

The rock of God is beneath our feet. Let us meet the
Archbishop with cordial thanksgiving:

Our lord, our Archbishop returns. And when the Archbishop returns

Our doubts are dispelled. Let us therefore rejoice,

I say rejoice, and show a glad face for his welcome.

I am the Archbishop's man. Let us give the Archbishop
welcome!

Third Priest

For good or ill, let the wheel turn.

The wheel has been still, these seven years, and no
good.

For ill or good, let the wheel turn.

For who knows the end of good or evil?

Until the grinders cease

And the door shall be shut in the street,

And all the daughters of music shall be brought low.

Chorus

Here is no continuing city, here is no abiding stay.

Ill the wind, ill the time, uncertain the profit, certain
the danger.

O late late late, late is the time, late too late, and rotten
the year;

Evil the wind, and bitter the sea, and grey the sky, grey
grey grey.

O Thomas, return, Archbishop; return, return to
France.

Return. Quickly. Quietly. Leave us to perish in quiet.
You come with applause, you come with rejoicing, but
    you come bringing death into Canterbury:
A doom on the house, a doom on yourself, a doom on
    the world.

We do not wish anything to happen.
Seven years we have lived quietly,
Succeeded in avoiding notice,
Living and partly living.
There have been oppression and luxury,
There have been poverty and licence,
There has been minor injustice.
Yet we have gone on living,
Living and partly living.
Sometimes the corn has failed us,
Sometimes the harvest is good,
One year is a year of rain,
Another a year of dryness,
One year the apples are abundant,
Another year the plums are lacking.
Yet we have gone on living,
Living and partly living.
We have kept the feasts, heard the masses,
We have brewed beer and cyder,
Gathered wood against the winter,
Talked at the corner of the fire,
Talked at the corners of streets,
Talked not always in whispers,
Living and partly living.

We have seen births, deaths and marriages,
We have had various scandals,
We have been afflicted with taxes,
We have had laughter and gossip,
Several girls have disappeared
Unaccountably, and some not able to.
We have all had our private terrors,
Our particular shadows, our secret fears.
But now a great fear is upon us, a fear not of one but
   of many,
A fear like birth and death, when we see birth and
   death alone
In a void apart. We
Are afraid in a fear which we cannot know, which we
   cannot face, which none understands,
And our hearts are torn from us, our brains unskinned
   like the layers of an onion, our selves are lost lost
In a final fear which none understands. O Thomas
   Archbishop,
O Thomas our Lord, leave us and leave us be, in our
   humble and tarnished frame of existence, leave
   us; do not ask us
To stand to the doom on the house, the doom on the
   Archbishop, the doom on the world.
Archbishop, secure and assured of your fate, unaffrayed
   among the shades, do you realise what you ask, do
   you realise what it means
To the small folk drawn into the pattern of fate, the
   small folk who live among small things,
The strain on the brain of the small folk who stand to

the doom of the house, the doom of their lord, the
doom of the world?

O Thomas, Archbishop, leave us, leave us, leave sullen Dover, and set sail for France. Thomas our
Archbishop still our Archbishop even in France.
Thomas Archbishop, set the white sail between
the grey sky and the bitter sea, leave us, leave us
for France.

SECOND PRIEST

What a way to talk at such a juncture!
You are foolish, immodest and babbling women.
Do you not know that the good Archbishop
Is likely to arrive at any moment?
The crowds in the streets will be cheering and cheering,
You go on croaking like frogs in the treetops:
But frogs at least can be cooked and eaten.
Whatever you are afraid of, in your craven apprehen-
sion,
Let me ask you at the least to put on pleasant faces,
And give a hearty welcome to our good Archbishop.
[*Enter* THOMAS.]

THOMAS

Peace. And let them be, in their exaltation.
They speak better than they know, and beyond your
understanding.
They know and do not know, what it is to act or suffer.
They know and do not know, that action is suffering
And suffering is action. Neither does the agent suffer
Nor the patient act. But both are fixed

In an eternal action, an eternal patience
To which all must consent that it may be willed
And which all must suffer that they may will it,
That the pattern may subsist, for the pattern is the
    action
And the suffering, that the wheel may turn and still
Be forever still.

Second Priest

O my Lord, forgive me, I did not see you coming,
Engrossed by the chatter of these foolish women.
Forgive us, my Lord, you would have had a better
    welcome
If we had been sooner prepared for the event.
But your Lordship knows that seven years of waiting,
Seven years of prayer, seven years of emptiness,
Have better prepared our hearts for your coming,
Than seven days could make ready Canterbury.
However, I will have fires laid in all your rooms
To take the chill off our English December,
Your Lordship now being used to a better climate.
Your Lordship will find your rooms in order as you
    left them.

Thomas

And will try to leave them in order as I find them.
I am more than grateful for all your kind attentions.
These are small matters. Little rest in Canterbury
With eager enemies restless about us.
Rebellious bishops, York, London, Salisbury,
Would have intercepted our letters,

Filled the coast with spies and sent to meet me
Some who hold me in bitterest hate.
By God's grace aware of their prevision
I sent my letters on another day,
Had fair crossing, found at Sandwich
Broc, Warenne, and the Sheriff of Kent,
Those who had sworn to have my head from me
Only John, the Dean of Salisbury,
Fearing for the King's name, warning against treason,
Made them hold their hands. So for the time
We are unmolested.

FIRST PRIEST
But do they follow after?

THOMAS
For a little time the hungry hawk
Will only soar and hover, circling lower,
Waiting excuse, pretence, opportunity.
End will be simple, sudden, God-given.
Meanwhile the substance of our first act
Will be shadows, and the strife with shadows.
Heavier the interval than the consummation.
All things prepare the event. Watch.
[*Enter* FIRST TEMPTER.]

FIRST TEMPTER
You see, my Lord, I do not wait upon ceremony:
Here I have come, forgetting all acrimony,
Hoping that your present gravity
Will find excuse for my humble levity

23

Remembering all the good time past.
Your Lordship won't despise an old friend out of
    favour?
Old Tom, gay Tom, Becket of London,
Your Lordship won't forget that evening on the river
When the King, and you and I were all friends to-
    gether?
Friendship should be more than biting Time can
    sever.
What, my Lord, now that you recover
Favour with the King, shall we say that summer's over
Or that the good time cannot last?
Fluting in the meadows, viols in the hall,
Laughter and apple-blossom floating on the water,
Singing at nightfall, whispering in chambers,
Fires devouring the winter season,
Eating up the darkness, with wit and wine and wisdom!
Now that the King and you are in amity,
Clergy and laity may return to gaiety,
Mirth and sportfulness need not walk warily.

THOMAS

You talk of seasons that are past. I remember
Not worth forgetting.

TEMPTER

            And of the new season.
Spring has come in winter. Snow in the branches
Shall float as sweet as blossoms. Ice along the ditches
Mirror the sunlight. Love in the orchard
Send the sap shooting. Mirth matches melancholy.

24

THOMAS

We do not know very much of the future
Except that from generation to generation
The same things happen again and again.
Men learn little from others' experience.
But in the life of one man, never
The same time returns. Sever
The cord, shed the scale. Only
The fool, fixed in his folly, may think
He can turn the wheel on which he turns.

TEMPTER

My Lord, a nod is as good as a wink.
A man will often love what he spurns.
For the good times past, that are come again
I am your man.

THOMAS

             Not in this train
Look to your behaviour. You were safer
Think of penitence and follow your master.

TEMPTER

Not at this gait!
If you go so fast, others may go faster.
Your Lordship is too proud!
The safest beast is not the one that roars most loud,
This was not the way of the King our master!
You were not used to be so hard upon sinners
When they were your friends. Be easy, man!
The easy man lives to eat the best dinners.

Take a friend's advice. Leave well alone,
Or your goose may be cooked and eaten to the bone.

THOMAS

You come twenty years too late.

TEMPTER

Then I leave you to your fate.
I leave you to the pleasures of your higher vices,
Which will have to be paid for at higher prices.
Farewell, my Lord, I do not wait upon ceremony,
I leave as I came, forgetting all acrimony,
Hoping that your present gravity
Will find excuse for my humble levity.
If you will remember me, my Lord, at your prayers,
I'll remember you at kissing-time below the stairs.

THOMAS

Leave-well-alone, the springtime fancy,
So one thought goes whistling down the wind.
The impossible is still temptation.
The impossible, the undesirable,
Voices under sleep, waking a dead world,
So that the mind may not be whole in the present.
[*Enter* SECOND TEMPTER.]

SECOND TEMPTER

Your Lordship has forgotten me, perhaps. I will re-
    mind you.
We met at Clarendon, at Northampton,
And last at Montmirail, in Maine. Now that I have
    recalled them,

Let us but set these not too pleasant memories
In balance against other, earlier
And weightier ones: those of the Chancellorship.
See how the late ones rise! You, master of policy
Whom all acknowledged, should guide the state again.

THOMAS

Your meaning?

TEMPTER

The Chancellorship that you resigned
When you were made Archbishop—that was a mistake
On your part—still may be regained. Think, my Lord,
Power obtained grows to glory,
Life lasting, a permanent possession.
A templed tomb, monument of marble.
Rule over men reckon no madness.

THOMAS

To the man of God what gladness?

TEMPTER

Sadness
Only to those giving love to God alone.
Shall he who held the solid substance
Wander waking with deceitful shadows?
Power is present. Holiness hereafter.

THOMAS

Who then?

TEMPTER

        The Chancellor. King and Chancellor.
King commands. Chancellor richly rules.
This is a sentence not taught in the schools.
To set down the great, protect the poor,
Beneath the throne of God can man do more?
Disarm the ruffian, strengthen the laws,
Rule for the good of the better cause,
Dispensing justice make all even,
Is thrive on earth, and perhaps in heaven.

THOMAS

What means?

TEMPTER

        Real power
Is purchased at price of a certain submission.
Your spiritual power is earthly perdition.
Power is present, for him who will wield.

THOMAS

Who shall have it?

TEMPTER

        He who will come.

THOMAS

What shall be the month?

TEMPTER

        The last from the first.

THOMAS

What shall we give for it?

TEMPTER
Pretence of priestly power.

THOMAS
Why should we give it?

TEMPTER
For the power and the glory.

THOMAS
No!

TEMPTER
Yes! Or bravery will be broken,
Cabined in Canterbury, realmless ruler,
Self-bound servant of a powerless Pope,
The old stag, circled with hounds.

THOMAS
No!

TEMPTER
Yes! men must manœuvre. Monarchs also,
Waging war abroad, need fast friends at home.
Private policy is public profit;
Dignity still shall be dressed with decorum.

THOMAS
You forget the bishops
Whom I have laid under excommunication.

TEMPTER
Hungry hatred
Will not strive against intelligent self-interest.

29

THOMAS

You forget the barons. Who will not forget
Constant curbing of petty privilege.

TEMPTER

Against the barons
Is King's cause, churl's cause, Chancellor's cause.

THOMAS

No! shall I, who keep the keys
Of heaven and hell, supreme alone in England,
Who bind and loose, with power from the Pope,
Descend to desire a punier power?
Delegate to deal the doom of damnation,
To condemn kings, not serve among their servants,
Is my open office. No! Go.

TEMPTER

Then I leave you to your fate.
Your sin soars sunward, covering kings' falcons.

THOMAS

Temporal power, to build a good world,
To keep order, as the world knows order.
Those who put their faith in worldly order
Not controlled by the order of God,
In confident ignorance, but arrest disorder,
Make it fast, breed fatal disease,
Degrade what they exalt. Power with the King—
I *was* the King, his arm, his better reason.
But what was once exaltation

Would now be only mean descent.
[*Enter* THIRD TEMPTER.]

THIRD TEMPTER

I am an unexpected visitor.

THOMAS

I expected you.

TEMPTER

But not in this guise, or for my present purpose.

THOMAS

No purpose brings surprise.

TEMPTER

Well, my Lord,
I am no trifler, and no politician.
To idle or intrigue at court
I have no skill. I am no courtier.
I know a horse, a dog, a wench;
I know how to hold my estates in order,
A country-keeping lord who minds his own business.
It is we country lords who know the country
And we who know what the country needs.
It is our country. We care for the country.
We are the backbone of the nation.
We, not the plotting parasites
About the King. Excuse my bluntness:
I am a rough straightforward Englishman.

THOMAS

Proceed straight forward.

TEMPTER

                Purpose is plain.
Endurance of friendship does not depend
Upon ourselves, but upon circumstance.
But circumstance is not undetermined.
Unreal friendship may turn to real
But real friendship, once ended, cannot be mended.
Sooner shall enmity turn to alliance.
The enmity that never knew friendship
Can sooner know accord.

THOMAS

                For a countryman
You wrap your meaning in as dark generality
As any courtier.

TEMPTER

                This is the simple fact!
You have no hope of reconciliation
With Henry the King. You look only
To blind assertion in isolation.
That is a mistake.

THOMAS

                O Henry, O my King!

TEMPTER

                                    Other friends
May be found in the present situation.
King in England is not all-powerful;
King is in France, squabbling in Anjou;
Round him waiting hungry sons.

We are for England. We are in England.
You and I, my Lord, are Normans.
England is a land for Norman
Sovereignty. Let the Angevin
Destroy himself, fighting in Anjou.
He does not understand us, the English barons.
We are the people.

THOMAS

To what does this lead?

TEMPTER

            To a happy coalition
Of intelligent interests.

THOMAS

            But what have you—
If you do speak for barons—

TEMPTER

            For a powerful party
Which has turned its eyes in your direction—
To gain from you, your Lordship asks.
For us, Church favour would be an advantage,
Blessing of Pope powerful protection
In the fight for liberty. You, my Lord,
In being with us, would fight a good stroke
At once, for England and for Rome,
Ending the tyrannous jurisdiction
Of king's court over bishop's court,
Of king's court over baron's court.

Thomas

Which I helped to found.

Tempter

Which you helped to found.
But time past is time forgotten.
We expect the rise of a new constellation.

Thomas

And if the Archbishop cannot trust the King,
How can he trust those who work for King's undoing?

Tempter

Kings will allow no power but their own;
Church and people have good cause against the throne.

Thomas

If the Archbishop cannot trust the Throne,
He has good cause to trust none but God alone.
I ruled once as Chancellor
And men like you were glad to wait at my door.
Not only in the court, but in the field
And in the tilt-yard I made many yield.
Shall I who ruled like an eagle over doves
Now take the shape of a wolf among wolves?
Pursue your treacheries as you have done before:
No one shall say that I betrayed a king.

Tempter

Then, my Lord, I shall not wait at your door.
And I well hope, before another spring
The King will show his regard for your loyalty.

THOMAS

To make, then break, this thought has come before,
The desperate exercise of failing power.
Samson in Gaza did no more.
But if I break, I must break myself alone.
[*Enter* FOURTH TEMPTER.]

FOURTH TEMPTER

Well done, Thomas, your will is hard to bend.
And with me beside you, you shall not lack a friend.

THOMAS

Who are you? I expected
Three visitors, not four.

TEMPTER

Do not be surprised to receive one more.
Had I been expected, I had been here before.
I always precede expectation.

THOMAS

Who are you?

TEMPTER

As you do not know me, I do not need a name,
And, as you know me, that is why I come.
You know me, but have never seen my face.
To meet before was never time or place.

THOMAS

Say what you come to say.

TEMPTER

It shall be said at last.
Hooks have been baited with morsels of the past.
Wantonness is weakness. As for the King,
His hardened hatred shall have no end.
You know truly, the King will never trust
Twice, the man who has been his friend.
Borrow use cautiously, employ
Your services as long as you have to lend.
You would wait for trap to snap
Having served your turn, broken and crushed.
As for barons, envy of lesser men
Is still more stubborn than king's anger.
Kings have public policy, barons private profit,
Jealousy raging possession of the fiend.
Barons are employable against each other;
Greater enemies must kings destroy.

THOMAS

What is your counsel?

TEMPTER

Fare forward to the end.
All other ways are closed to you
Except the way already chosen.
But what is pleasure, kingly rule,
Or rule of men beneath a king,
With craft in corners, stealthy stratagem,
To general grasp of spiritual power?
Man oppressed by sin, since Adam fell—
You hold the keys of heaven and hell.

Power to bind and loose: bind, Thomas, bind,
King and bishop under your heel.
King, emperor, bishop, baron, king:
Uncertain mastery of melting armies,
War, plague, and revolution,
New conspiracies, broken pacts;
To be master or servant within an hour,
This is the course of temporal power.
The Old King shall know it, when at last breath,
No sons, no empire, he bites broken teeth.
You hold the skein: wind, Thomas, wind
The thread of eternal life and death.
You hold this power, hold it.

THOMAS
                    Supreme, in this land?

TEMPTER
Supreme, but for one.

THOMAS
                    That I do not understand.

TEMPTER
It is not for me to tell you how this may be so;
I am only here, Thomas, to tell you what you know.

THOMAS
How long shall this be?

TEMPTER
Save what you know already, ask nothing of me.
But think, Thomas, think of glory after death.

When king is dead, there's another king,
And one more king is another reign.
King is forgotten, when another shall come:
Saint and Martyr rule from the tomb.
Think, Thomas, think of enemies dismayed,
Creeping in penance, frightened of a shade;
Think of pilgrims, standing in line
Before the glittering jewelled shrine,
From generation to generation
Bending the knee in supplication,
Think of the miracles, by God's grace,
And think of your enemies, in another place.

THOMAS

I have thought of these things.

TEMPTER

         That is why I tell you.
Your thoughts have more power than kings to compel
    you.
You have also thought, sometimes at your prayers,
Sometimes hesitating at the angles of stairs,
And between sleep and waking, early in the morning,
When the bird cries, have thought of further scorning.
That nothing lasts, but the wheel turns,
The nest is rifled, and the bird mourns;
That the shrine shall be pillaged, and the gold spent,
The jewels gone for light ladies' ornament,
The sanctuary broken, and its stores
Swept into the laps of parasites and whores.
When miracles cease, and the faithful desert you.

And men shall only do their best to forget you.
And later is worse, when men will not hate you
Enough to defame or to execrate you,
But pondering the qualities that you lacked
Will only try to find the historical fact.
When men shall declare that there was no mystery
About this man who played a certain part in history.

THOMAS

But what is there to do? What is left to be done?
Is there no enduring crown to be won?

TEMPTER

Yes, Thomas, yes; you have thought of that too.
What can compare with glory of Saints
Dwelling forever in presence of God?
What earthly glory, of king or emperor,
What earthly pride, that is not poverty
Compared with richness of heavenly grandeur?
Seek the way of martyrdom, make yourself the lowest
On earth, to be high in heaven.
And see far off below you, where the gulf is fixed,
Your persecutors, in timeless torment,
Parched passion, beyond expiation.

THOMAS

No!

Who are you, tempting with my own desires?
Others have come, temporal tempters,
With pleasure and power at palpable price.
What do you offer? What do you ask?

39

TEMPTER

I offer what you desire. I ask
What you have to give. Is it too much
For such a vision of eternal grandeur?

THOMAS

Others offered real goods, worthless
But real. You only offer
Dreams to damnation.

TEMPTER

You have often dreamt them.

THOMAS

Is there no way, in my soul's sickness,
Does not lead to damnation in pride?
I well know that these temptations
Mean present vanity and future torment.
Can sinful pride be driven out
Only by more sinful? Can I neither act nor suffer
Without perdition?

TEMPTER

You know and do not know, what it is to act or suffer.
You know and do not know, that action is suffering,
And suffering action. Neither does the agent suffer
Nor the patient act. But both are fixed
In an eternal action, an eternal patience
To which all must consent that it may be willed
And which all must suffer that they may will it,

That the pattern may subsist, that the wheel may turn
    and still
Be forever still.

Chorus
There is no rest in the house. There is no rest in the
    street.
I hear restless movement of feet. And the air is heavy
    and thick.
Thick and heavy the sky. And the earth presses up
    against our feet.
What is the sickly smell, the vapour? The dark green
    light from a cloud on a withered tree? The earth
    is heaving to parturition of issue of hell. What is
    the sticky dew that forms on the back of my hand?

The Four Tempters
Man's life is a cheat and a disappointment;
All things are unreal,
Unreal or disappointing:
The Catherine wheel, the pantomime cat,
The prizes given at the children's party,
The prize awarded for the English Essay,
The scholar's degree, the statesman's decoration.
All things become less real, man passes
From unreality to unreality.
This man is obstinate, blind, intent
On self-destruction.
Passing from deception to deception,
From grandeur to grandeur to final illusion,

Lost in the wonder of his own greatness,
The enemy of society, enemy of himself.

THE THREE PRIESTS

O Thomas my Lord do not fight the intractable tide,
Do not sail the irresistible wind; in the storm,
Should we not wait for the sea to subside, in the night
Abide the coming of day, when the traveller may find
    his way,
The sailor lay course by the sun?

CHORUS, PRIESTS and TEMPTERS alternately

C. Is it the owl that calls, or a signal between the
    trees?
P. Is the window-bar made fast, is the door under lock
    and bolt?
T. Is it rain that taps at the window, is it wind that
    pokes at the door?
C. Does the torch flame in the hall, the candle in the
    room?
P. Does the watchman walk by the wall?
T. Does the mastiff prowl by the gate?
C. Death has a hundred hands and walks by a thou-
    sand ways.
P. He may come in the sight of all, he may pass un-
    seen unheard.
T. Come whispering through the ear, or a sudden
    shock on the skull.
C. A man may walk with a lamp at night, and yet be
    drowned in a ditch.

P. A man may climb the stair in the day, and slip on
    a broken step.
T. A man may sit at meat, and feel the cold in his
    groin.

We have not been happy, my Lord, we have not been
    too happy.
We are not ignorant women, we know what we must
    expect and not expect.
We know of oppression and torture,
We know of extortion and violence,
Destitution, disease,
The old without fire in winter,
The child without milk in summer,
Our labour taken away from us,
Our sins made heavier upon us.
We have seen the young man mutilated,
The torn girl trembling by the mill-stream.
And meanwhile we have gone on living,
Living and partly living,
Picking together the pieces,
Gathering faggots at nightfall,
Building a partial shelter,
For sleeping, and eating and drinking and laughter.

God gave us always some reason, some hope; but now
    a new terror has soiled us, which none can avert,
    none can avoid, flowing under our feet and over
    the sky;

Under doors and down chimneys, flowing in at the ear
    and the mouth and the eye.
God is leaving us, God is leaving us, more pang, more
    pain than birth or death.
Sweet and cloying through the dark air
Falls the stifling scent of despair;
The forms take shape in the dark air:
Puss-purr of leopard, footfall of padding bear,
Palm-pat of nodding ape, square hyaena waiting
For laughter, laughter, laughter. The Lords of Hell
    are here.
They curl round you, lie at your feet, swing and wing
    through the dark air.
O Thomas Archbishop, save us, save us, save yourself
    that we may be saved;
Destroy yourself and we are destroyed.

THOMAS

Now is my way clear, now is the meaning plain:
Temptation shall not come in this kind again.
The last temptation is the greatest treason:
To do the right deed for the wrong reason.
The natural vigour in the venial sin
Is the way in which our lives begin.
Thirty years ago, I searched all the ways
That lead to pleasure, advancement and praise.
Delight in sense, in learning and in thought,
Music and philosophy, curiosity,
The purple bullfinch in the lilac tree,
The tilt-yard skill, the strategy of chess,

Love in the garden, singing to the instrument,
Were all things equally desirable.
Ambition comes when early force is spent
And when we find no longer all things possible.
Ambition comes behind and unobservable.
Sin grows with doing good. When I imposed the King's
    law
In England, and waged war with him against Toulouse,
I beat the barons at their own game. I
Could then despise the men who thought me most
    contemptible,
The raw nobility, whose manners matched their finger-
    nails.
While I ate out of the King's dish
To become servant of God was never my wish.
Servant of God has chance of greater sin
And sorrow, than the man who serves a king.
For those who serve the greater cause may make the
    cause serve them,
Still doing right: and striving with political men
May make that cause political, not by what they do
But by what they are. I know
What yet remains to show you of my history
Will seem to most of you at best futility,
Senseless self-slaughter of a lunatic,
Arrogant passion of a fanatic.
I know that history at all times draws
The strangest consequence from remotest cause.
But for every evil, every sacrilege,
Crime, wrong, oppression and the axe's edge,

Indifference, exploitation, you, and you,
And you, must all be punished. So must you.
I shall no longer act or suffer, to the sword's end.
Now my good Angel, whom God appoints
To be my guardian, hover over the swords' points.

Interlude

preaches in the Cathedral on Christmas Morning, 1170.

'Glory to God in the highest, and on earth peace to men of good will.' *The fourteenth verse of the second chapter of the Gospel according to Saint Luke.* In the Name of the Father, and of the Son, and of the Holy Ghost. Amen.

Dear children of God, my sermon this Christmas morning will be a very short one. I wish only that you should meditate in your hearts the deep meaning and mystery of our masses of Christmas Day. For whenever Mass is said, we re-enact the Passion and Death of Our Lord; and on this Christmas Day we do this in celebration of His Birth. So that at the same moment we rejoice in His coming for the salvation of men, and offer again to God His Body and Blood in sacrifice, oblation and satisfaction for the sins of the whole world. It was in this same night that has just passed, that a multitude of the heavenly host appeared before the shepherds at Bethlehem, saying 'Glory to God in the highest, and on earth peace to men of good will'; at this same time of all the year that we celebrate at once the Birth of Our Lord and His Passion and Death upon the Cross. Be-

47

loved, as the World sees, this is to behave in a strange fashion. For who in the World will both mourn and rejoice at once and for the same reason? For either joy will be overborne by mourning, or mourning will be cast out by joy; so it is only in these our Christian mysteries that we can rejoice and mourn at once for the same reason. Now think for a moment about the meaning of this word 'peace.' Does it seem strange to you that the angels should have announced Peace, when ceaselessly the world has been stricken with War and the fear of War? Does it seem to you that the angelic voices were mistaken, and that the promise was a disappointment and a cheat?

Reflect now, how Our Lord Himself spoke of Peace. He said to His disciples, 'My peace I leave with you, my peace I give unto you.' Did He mean peace as we think of it: the kingdom of England at peace with its neighbours, the barons at peace with the King, the householder counting over his peaceful gains, the swept hearth, his best wine for a friend at the table, his wife singing to the children? Those men His disciples knew no such things: they went forth to journey afar, to suffer by land and sea, to know torture, imprisonment, disappointment, to suffer death by martyrdom. What then did He mean? If you ask that, remember then that He said also, 'Not as the world gives, give I unto you.' So then, He gave to His disciples peace, but not peace as the world gives.

Consider also one thing of which you have probably never thought. Not only do we at the feast of Christmas celebrate at once Our Lord's Birth and His Death: but on the next day we celebrate the martyrdom of His first martyr, the blessed Stephen. Is it an accident, do you think, that the day of the first martyr follows immediately the day of the Birth of Christ? By no means. Just as we rejoice and mourn at once, in the Birth and in the Passion of Our Lord; so also, in a smaller figure, we both rejoice and mourn in the death of martyrs. We mourn, for the sins of the world that has martyred them; we rejoice, that another soul is numbered among the Saints in Heaven, for the glory of God and for the salvation of men.

Beloved, we do not think of a martyr simply as a good Christian who has been killed because he is a Christian: for that would be solely to mourn. We do not think of him simply as a good Christian who has been elevated to the company of the Saints: for that would be simply to rejoice: and neither our mourning nor our rejoicing is as the world's is. A Christian martyrdom is never an accident, for Saints are not made by accident. Still less is a Christian martyrdom the effect of a man's will to become a Saint, as a man by willing and contriving may become a ruler of men. A martyrdom is always the design of God, for His love of men, to warn them and to lead them, to bring them back to His ways. It is never the design of man; for the true martyr is he who has become the instrument of God, who has lost his will in the will of God, and who no longer desires anything for himself, not even the glory of being a martyr. So thus as on earth the

Church mourns and rejoices at once, in a fashion that the world cannot understand; so in Heaven the Saints are most high, having made themselves most low, and are seen, not as we see them, but in the light of the Godhead from which they draw their being.

I have spoken to you to-day, dear children of God, of the martyrs of the past, asking you to remember especially our martyr of Canterbury, the blessed Archbishop Elphege; because it is fitting, on Christ's birth day, to remember what is that Peace which He brought; and because, dear children, I do not think I shall ever preach to you again; and because it is possible that in a short time you may have yet another martyr, and that one perhaps not the last. I would have you keep in your hearts these words that I say, and think of them at another time. In the Name of the Father, and of the Son, and of the Holy Ghost. Amen.

Part II

★

Characters

THREE PRIESTS
FOUR KNIGHTS
ARCHBISHOP THOMAS BECKET
CHORUS OF WOMEN OF CANTERBURY
ATTENDANTS

The first scene is in the Archbishop's Hall,
the second scene is in the Cathedral,
on December 29th, 1170

Does the bird sing in the South?

Only the sea-bird cries, driven inland by the storm.

What sign of the spring of the year?

Only the death of the old: not a stir, not a shoot, not
a breath.

Do the days begin to lengthen?

Longer and darker the day, shorter and colder the
night.

Still and stifling the air: but a wind is stored up in the
East.

The starved crow sits in the field, attentive; and in the
wood

The owl rehearses the hollow note of death.

What signs of a bitter spring?

The wind stored up in the East.

What, at the time of the birth of Our Lord, at Christ-
mastide,

Is there not peace upon earth, goodwill among men?

The peace of this world is always uncertain, unless
men keep the peace of God.

And war among men defiles this world, but death in
the Lord renews it,

And the world must be cleaned in the winter, or we
    shall have only
A sour spring, a parched summer, an empty harvest.
Between Christmas and Easter what work shall be done?
The ploughman shall go out in March and turn the
    same earth
He has turned before, the bird shall sing the same song.
When the leaf is out on the tree, when the elder and
    may
Burst over the stream, and the air is clear and high,
And voices trill at windows, and children tumble in
    front of the door,
What work shall have been done, what wrong
Shall the bird's song cover, the green tree cover, what
    wrong
Shall the fresh earth cover? We wait, and the time is
    short
But waiting is long.

[*Enter the* FIRST PRIEST *with a banner of St. Stephen
borne before him. The lines sung are in italics.*]

FIRST PRIEST

Since Christmas a day: and the day of St. Stephen, First
    Martyr.
*Princes moreover did sit, and did witness falsely against
    me.*
A day that was always most dear to the Archbishop
    Thomas.
And he kneeled down and cried with a loud voice:

54

Lord, lay not this sin to their charge.

Princes moreover did sit.

> [*Introit of St. Stephen is heard.*]
> [*Enter the* SECOND PRIEST, *with a banner of St. John the Apostle borne before him.*]

SECOND PRIEST

Since St. Stephen a day: and the day of St. John the
    Apostle.

In the midst of the congregation he opened his mouth.

That which was from the beginning, which we have
    heard,

Which we have seen with our eyes, and our hands have
    handled

Of the word of life; that which we have seen and heard

Declare we unto you.

In the midst of the congregation.

> [*Introit of St. John is heard.*]
> [*Enter the* THIRD PRIEST, *with a banner of the Holy Innocents borne before him.*]

THIRD PRIEST

Since St. John the Apostle a day: and the day of the
    Holy Innocents.

Out of the mouth of very babes, O God.

As the voice of many waters, of thunder, of harps,

They sung as it were a new song.

The blood of thy saints have they shed like water,

And there was no man to bury them. Avenge, O Lord,

The blood of thy saints. In Rama, a voice heard,
    weeping.

Out of the mouth of very babes, O God!
[THE PRIESTS *stand together with the banners behind them.*]

FIRST PRIEST

Since the Holy Innocents a day: the fourth day from Christmas.

THE THREE PRIESTS

Rejoice we all, keeping holy day.

FIRST PRIEST

As for the people, so also for himself, he offereth for sins.

He lays down his life for the sheep.

THE THREE PRIESTS

Rejoice we all, keeping holy day.

FIRST PRIEST

To-day?

SECOND PRIEST

To-day, what is to-day? For the day is half gone.

FIRST PRIEST

To-day, what is to-day? But another day, the dusk of the year.

SECOND PRIEST

To-day, what is to-day? Another night, and another dawn.

THIRD PRIEST

What day is the day that we know that we hope for
 or fear for?
Every day is the day we should fear from or hope from.
 One moment
Weighs like another. Only in retrospection, selection,
We say, that was the day. The critical moment
That is always now, and here. Even now, in sordid
 particulars
The eternal design may appear.

[*Enter the* FOUR KNIGHTS. *The banners disappear.*]

FIRST KNIGHT

Servants of the King.

FIRST PRIEST

                    And known to us.
You are welcome. Have you ridden far?

FIRST KNIGHT

Not far to-day, but matters urgent
Have brought us from France. We rode hard,
Took ship yesterday, landed last night,
Having business with the Archbishop.

SECOND KNIGHT

Urgent business.

THIRD KNIGHT

From the King.

SECOND KNIGHT

By the King's order.

FIRST KNIGHT
Our men are outside.

FIRST PRIEST
You know the Archbishop's hospitality.
We are about to go to dinner.
The good Archbishop would be vexed
If we did not offer you entertainment
Before your business. Please dine with us.
Your men shall be looked after also.
Dinner before business. Do you like roast pork?

FIRST KNIGHT
Business before dinner. We will roast your pork
First, and dine upon it after.

SECOND KNIGHT
We must see the Archbishop.

THIRD KNIGHT
                    Go, tell the Archbishop
We have no need of his hospitality.
We will find our own dinner.

FIRST PRIEST [to attendant]
Go, tell His Lordship.

FOURTH KNIGHT
        How much longer will you keep us waiting?
[Enter THOMAS.]

THOMAS [to PRIESTS]
However certain our expectation

The moment foreseen may be unexpected
When it arrives. It comes when we are
Engrossed with matters of other urgency.
On my table you will find
The papers in order, and the documents signed.
[*To* KNIGHTS.]
You are welcome, whatever your business may be.
You say, from the King?

FIRST KNIGHT
                    Most surely from the King.
We must speak with you alone.

THOMAS [*to* PRIESTS]
                    Leave us then alone.
Now what is the matter?

FIRST KNIGHT
                    This is the matter.

THE THREE KNIGHTS
You are the Archbishop in revolt against the King; in
    rebellion to the King and the law of the land;
You are the Archbishop who was made by the King;
    whom he set in your place to carry out his com-
    mand.
You are his servant, his tool, and his jack,
You wore his favours on your back,
You had your honours all from his hand; from him you
    had the power, the seal and the ring.
This is the man who was the tradesman's son: the back-
    stairs brat who was born in Cheapside;

This is the creature that crawled upon the King;
   swollen with blood and swollen with pride.
Creeping out of the London dirt,
Crawling up like a louse on your shirt,
The man who cheated, swindled, lied; broke his oath
   and betrayed his King.

THOMAS

This is not true.
Both before and after I received the ring
I have been a loyal subject to the King.
Saving my order, I am at his command,
As his most faithful vassal in the land.

FIRST KNIGHT

Saving your order! let your order save you—
As I do not think it is like to do.
Saving your ambition is what you mean,
Saving your pride, envy and spleen.

SECOND KNIGHT

Saving your insolence and greed.
Won't you ask us to pray to God for you, in your need?

THIRD KNIGHT

Yes, we'll pray for you!

FIRST KNIGHT

Yes, we'll pray for you!

THE THREE KNIGHTS

Yes, we'll pray that God may help you!

THOMAS

But, gentlemen, your business
Which you said so urgent, is it only
Scolding and blaspheming?

FIRST KNIGHT
That was only
Our indignation, as loyal subjects.

THOMAS

Loyal? To whom?

FIRST KNIGHT
To the King!

SECOND KNIGHT
The King!

THIRD KNIGHT
The King!

THE THREE KNIGHTS
God bless him!

THOMAS

Then let your new coat of loyalty be worn
Carefully, so it get not soiled or torn.
Have you something to say?

FIRST KNIGHT
By the King's command.
Shall we say it now?

SECOND KNIGHT
Without delay,
Before the old fox is off and away.

THOMAS
What you have to say
By the King's command—if it be the King's command—
Should be said in public. If you make charges,
Then in public I will refute them.

FIRST KNIGHT
No! here and now!
[*They make to attack him, but the priests and attend-
ants return and quietly interpose themselves.*]

THOMAS
Now and here!

FIRST KNIGHT
Of your earlier misdeeds I shall make no mention.
They are too well known. But after dissension
Had ended, in France, and you were endued
With your former privilege, how did you show your
gratitude?
You had fled from England, not exiled
Or threatened, mind you; but in the hope
Of stirring up trouble in the French dominions.
You sowed strife abroad, you reviled
The King to the King of France, to the Pope,
Raising up against him false opinions.

SECOND KNIGHT

Yet the King, out of his charity,
And urged by your friends, offered clemency,
Made a pact of peace, and all dispute ended
Sent you back to your See as you demanded.

THIRD KNIGHT

And burying the memory of your transgressions
Restored your honours and your possessions.
All was granted for which you sued:
Yet how, I repeat, did you show your gratitude?

FIRST KNIGHT

Suspending those who had crowned the young prince,
Denying the legality of his coronation.

SECOND KNIGHT

Binding with the chains of anathema.

THIRD KNIGHT

Using every means in your power to evince
The King's faithful servants, every one who transacts
His business in his absence, the business of the nation.

FIRST KNIGHT

These are the facts.
Say therefore if you will be content
To answer in the King's presence. Therefore were we
    sent.

THOMAS

Never was it my wish
To uncrown the King's son, or to diminish

His honour and power. Why should he wish
To deprive my people of me and keep me from my own
And bid me sit in Canterbury, alone?
I would wish him three crowns rather than one,
And as for the bishops, it is not my yoke
That is laid upon them, or mine to revoke.
Let them go to the Pope. It was he who condemned
   them.

FIRST KNIGHT
Through you they were suspended.

SECOND KNIGHT
                    By you be this amended.

THIRD KNIGHT
Absolve them.

FIRST KNIGHT
   Absolve them.

THOMAS
                    I do not deny
That this was done through me. But it is not I
Who can loose whom the Pope has bound.
Let them go to him, upon whom redounds
Their contempt towards me, their contempt towards
   the Church shown.

FIRST KNIGHT
Be that as it may, here is the King's command:
That you and your servants depart from this land.

64

THOMAS

If that *is* the King's command, I will be bold
To say: seven years were my people without
My presence; seven years of misery and pain.
Seven years a mendicant on foreign charity
I lingered abroad: seven years is no brevity.
I shall not get those seven years back again.
Never again, you must make no doubt,
Shall the sea run between the shepherd and his fold.

FIRST KNIGHT

The King's justice, the King's majesty,
You insult with gross indignity;
Insolent madman, whom nothing deters
From attainting his servants and ministers.

THOMAS

It is not I who insult the King,
And there is higher than I or the King.
It is not I, Becket from Cheapside,
It is not against me, Becket, that you strive.
It is not Becket who pronounces doom,
But the Law of Christ's Church, the judgement of
    Rome.

FIRST KNIGHT

Priest, you have spoken in peril of your life.

SECOND KNIGHT

Priest, you have spoken in danger of the knife.

THIRD KNIGHT
Priest, you have spoken treachery and treason.

THE THREE KNIGHTS
Priest! traitor, confirmed in malfeasance.

THOMAS
I submit my cause to the judgement of Rome.
But if you kill me, I shall rise from my tomb
To submit my cause before God's throne.

[*Exit.*]

FOURTH KNIGHT
Priest! monk! and servant! take, hold, detain,
Restrain this man, in the King's name.

FIRST KNIGHT
Or answer with your bodies.

SECOND KNIGHT
                Enough of words.

THE FOUR KNIGHTS
We come for the King's justice, we come with swords.

[*Exeunt.*]

CHORUS
I have smelt them, the death-bringers, senses are quick-
    ened
By subtile forebodings; I have heard
Fluting in the night-time, fluting and owls, have seen
    at noon
Scaly wings slanting over, huge and ridiculous. I have
    tasted

The savour of putrid flesh in the spoon. I have felt

The heaving of earth at nightfall, restless, absurd. I
have heard

Laughter in the noises of beasts that make strange
noises: jackal, jackass, jackdaw; the scurrying noise
of mouse and jerboa; the laugh of the loon, the
lunatic bird. I have seen

Grey necks twisting, rat tails twining, in the thick light
of dawn. I have eaten

Smooth creatures still living, with the strong salt taste
of living things under sea; I have tasted

The living lobster, the crab, the oyster, the whelk and
the prawn; and they live and spawn in my bowels,
and my bowels dissolve in the light of dawn. I
have smelt

Death in the rose, death in the hollyhock, sweet pea,
hyacinth, primrose and cowslip. I have seen

Trunk and horn, tusk and hoof, in odd places;

I have lain on the floor of the sea and breathed with
the breathing of the sea-anemone, swallowed with
ingurgitation of the sponge. I have lain in the soil
and criticised the worm. In the air

Flirted with the passage of the kite, I have plunged with
the kite and cowered with the wren. I have felt

The horn of the beetle, the scale of the viper, the mobile
hard insensitive skin of the elephant, the evasive
flank of the fish. I have smelt

Corruption in the dish, incense in the latrine, the sewer
in the incense, the smell of sweet soap in the wood-

path, a hellish sweet scent in the woodpath, while
    the ground heaved. I have seen
Rings of light coiling downwards, descending
To the horror of the ape. Have I not known, not known
What was coming to be? It was here, in the kitchen, in
    the passage,
In the mews in the barn in the byre in the market-place
In our veins our bowels our skulls as well
As well as in the plottings of potentates
As well as in the consultations of powers.
What is woven on the loom of fate
What is woven in the councils of princes
Is woven also in our veins, our brains,
Is woven like a pattern of living worms
In the guts of the women of Canterbury.

I have smelt them, the death-bringers; now is too late
For action, too soon for contrition.
Nothing is possible but the shamed swoon
Of those consenting to the last humiliation.
I have consented, Lord Archbishop, have consented.
Am torn away, subdued, violated,
United to the spiritual flesh of nature,
Mastered by the animal powers of spirit,
Dominated by the lust of self-demolition,
By the final utter uttermost death of spirit,
By the final ecstasy of waste and shame,
O Lord Archbishop, O Thomas Archbishop, forgive us,
    forgive us, pray for us that we may pray for you,
    out of our shame.
[*Enter* THOMAS.]
68

THOMAS

Peace, and be at peace with your thoughts and visions.
These things had to come to you and you to accept them.
This is your share of the eternal burden,
The perpetual glory. This is one moment,
But know that another
Shall pierce you with a sudden painful joy
When the figure of God's purpose is made complete.
You shall forget these things, toiling in the household,
You shall remember them, droning by the fire,
When age and forgetfulness sweeten memory
Only like a dream that has often been told
And often been changed in the telling. They will seem
    unreal.
Human kind cannot bear very much reality.
[*Enter* PRIESTS.]

PRIESTS [*severally*]

My Lord, you must not stop here. To the minster.
Through the cloister. No time to waste. They are com-
    ing back, armed. To the altar, to the altar.

THOMAS

All my life they have been coming, these feet. All my life
I have waited. Death will come only when I am worthy,
And if I am worthy, there is no danger.
I have therefore only to make perfect my will.

PRIESTS

My Lord, they are coming. They will break through
    presently.

69

You will be killed. Come to the altar.
Make haste, my Lord. Don't stop here talking. It is not
    right.
What shall become of us, my Lord, if you are killed;
    what shall become of us?

THOMAS

Peace! be quiet! remember where you are, and what is
    happening;
No life here is sought for but mine,
And I am not in danger: only near to death.

PRIESTS

My Lord, to vespers! You must not be absent from
    vespers. You must not be absent from the divine
    office. To vespers. Into the cathedral!

THOMAS

Go to vespers, remember me at your prayers.
They shall find the shepherd here; the flock shall be
    spared.
I have had a tremour of bliss, a wink of heaven, a
    whisper,
And I would no longer be denied; all things
Proceed to a joyful consummation.

PRIESTS

Seize him! force him! drag him!

THOMAS

Keep your hands off!

70

PRIESTS

To vespers! Hurry.

[*They drag him off. While the* CHORUS *speak, the scene is changed to the cathedral.*]

CHORUS [*While a* Dies Iræ *is sung in Latin by a choir in the distance.*]

Numb the hand and dry the eyelid,
Still the horror, but more horror
Than when tearing in the belly.

Still the horror, but more horror
Than when twisting in the fingers,
Than when splitting in the skull.

More than footfall in the passage,
More than shadow in the doorway,
More than fury in the hall.

The agents of hell disappear, the human, they shrink
    and dissolve
Into dust on the wind, forgotten, unmemorable; only
    is here
The white flat face of Death, God's silent servant,
And behind the face of Death the Judgement
And behind the Judgement the Void, more horrid than
    active shapes of hell;
Emptiness, absence, separation from God;
The horror of the effortless journey, to the empty land
Which is no land, only emptiness, absence, the Void,

71

Where those who were men can no longer turn the
        mind
To distraction, delusion, escape into dream, pretence,
Where the soul is no longer deceived, for there are no
        objects, no tones,
No colours, no forms to distract, to divert the soul
From seeing itself, foully united forever, nothing with
        nothing,
Not what we call death, but what beyond death is not
        death,
We fear, we fear. Who shall then plead for me,
Who intercede for me, in my most need?

Dead upon the tree, my Saviour,
Let not be in vain Thy labour;
Help me, Lord, in my last fear.

Dust I am, to dust am bending,
From the final doom impending
Help me, Lord, for death is near.

[*In the cathedral.* THOMAS *and* PRIESTS.]

PRIESTS

Bar the door. Bar the door.
The door is barred.
We are safe. We are safe.
They dare not break in.
They cannot break in. They have not the force.
We are safe. We are safe.

72

THOMAS

Unbar the doors! throw open the doors!
I will not have the house of prayer, the church of Christ,
The sanctuary, turned into a fortress.
The Church shall protect her own, in her own way, not
As oak and stone; stone and oak decay,
Give no stay, but the Church shall endure.
The church shall be open, even to our enemies. Open
    the door!

PRIEST

My Lord! these are not men, these come not as men
    come, but
Like maddened beasts. They come not like men, who
Respect the sanctuary, who kneel to the Body of Christ,
But like beasts. You would bar the door
Against the lion, the leopard, the wolf or the boar,
Why not more
Against beasts with the souls of damned men, against
    men
Who would damn themselves to beasts. My Lord! My
    Lord!

THOMAS

You think me reckless, desperate and mad.
You argue by results, as this world does,
To settle if an act be good or bad.
You defer to the fact. For every life and every act
Consequence of good and evil can be shown.
And as in time results of many deeds are blended
So good and evil in the end become confounded.

It is not in time that my death shall be known;
It is out of time that my decision is taken
If you call that decision
To which my whole being gives entire consent.
I give my life
To the Law of God above the Law of Man.
Unbar the door! unbar the door!
We are not here to triumph by fighting, by stratagem,
    or by resistance,
Not to fight with beasts as men. We have fought the
    beast
And have conquered. We have only to conquer
Now, by suffering. This is the easier victory.
Now is the triumph of the Cross, now
Open the door! I command it. OPEN THE DOOR!

[*The door is opened. The* KNIGHTS *enter, slightly tipsy.*]

PRIESTS

This way, my Lord! Quick. Up the stair. To the roof.
    To the crypt. Quick. Come. Force him.

KNIGHTS

Where is Becket, the traitor to the King?
    Where is Becket, the meddling priest?
Come down Daniel to the lions' den,
    Come down Daniel for the mark of the beast.

Are you washed in the blood of the Lamb?
    Are you marked with the mark of the beast?
Come down Daniel to the lions' den,
    Come down Daniel and join in the feast.

74

Where is Becket the Cheapside brat?
  Where is Becket the faithless priest?
Come down Daniel to the lions' den,
  Come down Daniel and join in the feast.

THOMAS

It is the just man who
Like a bold lion, should be without fear.
I am here.
No traitor to the King. I am a priest,
A Christian, saved by the blood of Christ,
Ready to suffer with my blood.
This is the sign of the Church always,
The sign of blood. Blood for blood.
His blood given to buy my life,
My blood given to pay for His death,
My death for His death.

FIRST KNIGHT

Absolve all those you have excommunicated.

SECOND KNIGHT

Resign the powers you have arrogated.

THIRD KNIGHT

Restore to the King the money you appropriated.

FIRST KNIGHT

Renew the obedience you have violated.

THOMAS

For my Lord I am now ready to die,
That His Church may have peace and liberty.

Do with me as you will, to your hurt and shame;
But none of my people, in God's name,
Whether layman or clerk, shall you touch.
This I forbid.

KNIGHTS

Traitor! traitor! traitor!

THOMAS

You, Reginald, three times traitor you:
Traitor to me as my temporal vassal,
Traitor to me as your spiritual lord,
Traitor to God in desecrating His Church.

FIRST KNIGHT

No faith do I owe to a renegade,
And what I owe shall now be paid.

THOMAS

Now to Almighty God, to the Blessed Mary ever
Virgin, to the blessed John the Baptist, the holy apos-
tles Peter and Paul, to the blessed martyr Denys, and
to all the Saints, I commend my cause and that of the
Church.

While the KNIGHTS *kill him, we hear the*
CHORUS

Clear the air! clean the sky! wash the wind! take stone
    from stone and wash them.
The land is foul, the water is foul, our beasts and our-
    selves defiled with blood.
A rain of blood has blinded my eyes. Where is Eng-
    land? Where is Kent? Where is Canterbury?

76

O far far far far in the past; and I wander in a land
   of barren boughs: if I break them, they bleed; I
   wander in a land of dry stones: if I touch them
   they bleed.
How how can I ever return, to the soft quiet seasons?
Night stay with us, stop sun, hold season, let the day
   not come, let the spring not come.
Can I look again at the day and its common things,
   and see them all smeared with blood, through a
   curtain of falling blood?
We did not wish anything to happen.
We understood the private catastrophe,
The personal loss, the general misery,
Living and partly living;
The terror by night that ends in daily action,
The terror by day that ends in sleep;
But the talk in the market-place, the hand on the
   broom,
The night-time heaping of the ashes,
The fuel laid on the fire at daybreak,
These acts marked a limit to our suffering.
Every horror had its definition,
Every sorrow had a kind of end:
In life there is not time to grieve long.
But this, this is out of life, this is out of time,
An instant eternity of evil and wrong.
We are soiled by a filth that we cannot clean, united
   to supernatural vermin,
It is not we alone, it is not the house, it is not the city
   that is defiled,

77

But the world that is wholly foul.

Clear the air! clean the sky! wash the wind! take the
stone from the stone, take the skin from the arm,
take the muscle from the bone, and wash them.
Wash the stone, wash the bone, wash the brain,
wash the soul, wash them wash them!

[*The* KNIGHTS, *having completed the murder, advance
to the front of the stage and address the audience.*]

FIRST KNIGHT

We beg you to give us your attention for a few mo-
ments. We know that you may be disposed to judge
unfavourably of our action. You are Englishmen, and
therefore you believe in fair play: and when you see
one man being set upon by four, then your sympathies
are all with the under dog. I respect such feelings, I
share them. Nevertheless, I appeal to your sense of
honour. You are Englishmen, and therefore will not
judge anybody without hearing both sides of the case.
That is in accordance with our long-established prin-
ciple of Trial by Jury. I am not myself qualified to put
our case to you. I am a man of action and not of words.
For that reason I shall do no more than introduce the
other speakers, who, with their various abilities, and
different points of view, will be able to lay before you
the merits of this extremely complex problem. I shall
call upon our eldest member to speak first, my neigh-
bour in the country: Baron William de Traci.

THIRD KNIGHT

I am afraid I am not anything like such an experienced speaker as my old friend Reginald Fitz Urse would lead you to believe. But there is one thing I should like to say, and I might as well say it at once. It is this: in what we have done, and whatever you may think of it, we have been perfectly disinterested. [*The other* KNIGHTS: 'Hear! hear!'.] *We* are not getting anything out of this. We have much more to lose than to gain. We are four plain Englishmen who put our country first. I dare say that we didn't make a very good impression when we came in just now. The fact is that we knew we had taken on a pretty stiff job; I'll only speak for myself, but I had drunk a good deal— I am not a drinking man ordinarily—to brace myself up for it. When you come to the point, it does go against the grain to kill an Archbishop, especially when you have been brought up in good Church traditions. So if we seemed a bit rowdy, you will understand why it was; and for my part I am awfully sorry about it. We realised this was our duty, but all the same we had to work ourselves up to it. And, as I said, *we* are not getting a penny out of this. We know perfectly well how things will turn out. King Henry—God bless him—will have to say, for reasons of state, that he never meant this to happen; and there is going to be an awful row; and at the best we shall have to spend the rest of our lives abroad. And even when reasonable people come to see that the Archbishop *had* to be put out of the way—and personally I had a tremendous admiration for him—you must have noticed what a good show he put up at the end—they won't give *us* any glory.

No, we have done for ourselves, there's no mistake about that. So, as I said at the beginning, please give us at least the credit for being completely disinterested in this business. I think that is about all I have to say.

First Knight

I think we will all agree that William de Traci has spoken well and has made a very important point. The gist of his argument is this: that we have been completely disinterested. But our act itself needs more justification than that; and you must hear our other speakers. I shall next call upon Hugh de Morville, who has made a special study of statecraft and constitutional law. Sir Hugh de Morville.

Second Knight

I should like first to recur to a point that was very well put by our leader, Reginald Fitz Urse: that you are Englishmen, and therefore your sympathies are always with the under dog. It is the English spirit of fair play. Now the worthy Archbishop, whose good qualities I very much admired, has throughout been presented as the under dog. But is this really the case? I am going to appeal not to your emotions but to your reason. You are hard-headed sensible people, as I can see, and not to be taken in by emotional clap-trap. I therefore ask you to consider soberly: what were the Archbishop's aims? And what are King Henry's aims? In the answer to these questions lies the key to the problem.

The King's aim has been perfectly consistent. Dur-

ing the reign of the late Queen Matilda and the irrup-
tion of the unhappy usurper Stephen, the kingdom was
very much divided. Our King saw that the one thing
needful was to restore order: to curb the excessive
powers of local government, which were usually exer-
cised for selfish and often for seditious ends, and to
reform the legal system. He therefore intended that
Becket, who had proved himself an extremely able
administrator—no one denies that—should unite the
offices of Chancellor and Archbishop. Had Becket con-
curred with the King's wishes, we should have had an
almost ideal State: a union of spiritual and temporal
administration, under the central government. I knew
Becket well, in various official relations; and I may say
that I have never known a man so well qualified for
the highest rank of the Civil Service. And what hap-
pened? The moment that Becket. at the King's in-
stance, had been made Archbishop, he resigned the
office of Chancellor, he became more priestly than the
priests, he ostentatiously and offensively adopted an
ascetic manner of life, he affirmed immediately that
there was a higher order than that which our King,
and he as the King's servant, had for so many years
striven to establish; and that—God knows why—the two
orders were incompatible.

You will agree with me that such interference by an
Archbishop offends the instincts of a people like ours.
So far, I know that I have your approval: I read it in
your faces. It is only with the measures we have had to
adopt, in order to set matters to rights, that you take

81

issue. No one regrets the necessity for violence more than we do. Unhappily, there are times when violence is the only way in which social justice can be secured. At another time, you would condemn an Archbishop by vote of Parliament and execute him formally as a traitor, and no one would have to bear the burden of being called murderer. And at a later time still, even such temperate measures as these would become unnecessary. But, if you have now arrived at a just subordination of the pretensions of the Church to the welfare of the State, remember that it is we who took the first step. We have been instrumental in bringing about the state of affairs that you approve. We have served your interests; we merit your applause; and if there is any guilt whatever in the matter, you must share it with us.

FIRST KNIGHT

Morville has given us a great deal to think about. It seems to me that he has said almost the last word, for those who have been able to follow his very subtle reasoning. We have, however, one more speaker, who has I think another point of view to express. If there are any who are still unconvinced, I think that Richard Brito, coming as he does of a family distinguished for its loyalty to the Church, will be able to convince them. Richard Brito.

FOURTH KNIGHT

The speakers who have preceded me, to say nothing of our leader, Reginald Fitz Urse, have all spoken very

82

much to the point. I have nothing to add along their particular lines of argument. What I have to say may be put in the form of a question: *Who killed the Archbishop?* As you have been eye-witnesses of this lamentable scene, you may feel some surprise at my putting it in this way. But consider the course of events. I am obliged, very briefly, to go over the ground traversed by the last speaker. While the late Archbishop was Chancellor, no one, under the King, did more to weld the country together, to give it the unity, the stability, order, tranquillity, and justice that it so badly needed. From the moment he became Archbishop, he completely reversed his policy; he showed himself to be utterly indifferent to the fate of the country, to be, in fact, a monster of egotism. This egotism grew upon him, until it became at last an undoubted mania. I have unimpeachable evidence to the effect that before he left France he clearly prophesied, in the presence of numerous witnesses, that he had not long to live, and that he would be killed in England. He used every means of provocation; from his conduct, step by step, there can be no inference except that he had determined upon a death by martyrdom. Even at the last, he could have given us reason: you have seen how he evaded our questions. And when he had deliberately exasperated us beyond human endurance, he could still have easily escaped; he could have kept himself from us long enough to allow our righteous anger to cool. That was just what he did not wish to happen; he insisted, while we were still inflamed with wrath, that the doors should be opened. Need I say more? I think, with these facts before you, you will unhesitatingly render a verdict of Suicide while of Unsound Mind. It is the only charitable verdict you can give, upon one who was, after all, a great man.

First Knight

Thank you, Brito, I think that there is no more to be said; and I suggest that you now disperse quietly to your homes. Please be careful not to loiter in groups at street corners, and do nothing that might provoke any public outbreak.

[*Exeunt* Knights.]

First Priest

O father, father, gone from us, lost to us,
How shall we find you, from what far place
Do you look down on us? You now in Heaven,
Who shall now guide us, protect us, direct us?
After what journey through what further dread
Shall we recover your presence? When inherit
Your strength? The Church lies bereft,
Alone, desecrated, desolated, and the heathen shall
    build on the ruins,
Their world without God. I see it. I see it.

Third Priest

No. For the Church is stronger for this action,
Triumphant in adversity. It is fortified
By persecution: supreme, so long as men will die for it.
Go, weak sad men, lost erring souls, homeless in earth
    or heaven.

Go where the sunset reddens the last grey rock
Of Brittany, or the Gates of Hercules.
Go venture shipwreck on the sullen coasts
Where blackamoors make captive Christian men;
Go to the northern seas confined with ice
Where the dead breath makes numb the hand, makes
    dull the brain;
Find an oasis in the desert sun,
Go seek alliance with the heathen Saracen,
To share his filthy rites, and try to snatch
Forgetfulness in his libidinous courts,
Oblivion in the fountain by the date-tree;
Or sit and bite your nails in Aquitaine.
In the small circle of pain within the skull
You still shall tramp and tread one endless round
Of thought, to justify your action to yourselves,
Weaving a fiction which unravels as you weave,
Pacing forever in the hell of make-believe
Which never is belief: this is your fate on earth
And we must think no further of you.

FIRST PRIEST

                     O my lord
The glory of whose new state is hidden from us,
Pray for us of your charity.

SECOND PRIEST

                 Now in the sight of God
Conjoined with all the saints and martyrs gone before
    you,
Remember us.

THIRD PRIEST

Let our thanks ascend

To God, who has given us another Saint in Canterbury.

CHORUS [*While a* Te Deum *is sung in Latin by a choir in the distance.*]

We praise Thee, O God, for Thy glory displayed in all the creatures of the earth,

In the snow, in the rain, in the wind, in the storm; in all of Thy creatures, both the hunters and the hunted.

For all things exist only as seen by Thee, only as known by Thee, all things exist

Only in Thy light, and Thy glory is declared even in that which denies Thee; the darkness declares the glory of light.

Those who deny Thee could not deny, if Thou didst not exist; and their denial is never complete, for if it were so, they would not exist.

They affirm Thee in living; all things affirm Thee in living; the bird in the air, both the hawk and the finch; the beast on the earth, both the wolf and the lamb; the worm in the soil and the worm in the belly.

Therefore man, whom Thou hast made to be conscious of Thee, must consciously praise Thee, in thought and in word and in deed.

Even with the hand to the broom, the back bent in laying the fire, the knee bent in cleaning the hearth, we, the scrubbers and sweepers of Canterbury,

The back bent under toil, the knee bent under sin, the
   hands to the face under fear, the head bent under
   grief,
Even in us the voices of seasons, the snuffle of winter,
   the song of spring, the drone of summer, the
   voices of beasts and of birds, praise Thee.
We thank Thee for Thy mercies of blood, for Thy
   redemption by blood. For the blood of Thy martyrs and saints
Shall enrich the earth, shall create the holy places.
For wherever a saint has dwelt, wherever a martyr has
   given his blood for the blood of Christ,
There is holy ground, and the sanctity shall not depart
   from it
Though armies trample over it, though sightseers come
   with guide-books looking over it;
From where the western seas gnaw at the coast of Iona,
To the death in the desert, the prayer in forgotten
   places by the broken imperial column,
From such ground springs that which forever renews
   the earth
Though it is forever denied. Therefore, O God, we
   thank Thee
Who hast given such blessing to Canterbury.

Forgive us, O Lord, we acknowledge ourselves as type
   of the common man,
Of the men and women who shut the door and sit by
   the fire;
Who fear the blessing of God, the loneliness of the

night of God, the surrender required, the deprivation inflicted;

Who fear the injustice of men less than the justice of God;

Who fear the hand at the window, the fire in the thatch, the fist in the tavern, the push into the canal,

Less than we fear the love of God.

We acknowledge our trespass, our weakness, our fault; we acknowledge

That the sin of the world is upon our heads; that the blood of the martyrs and the agony of the saints

Is upon our heads.

Lord, have mercy upon us.

Christ, have mercy upon us.

Lord, have mercy upon us.

Blessed Thomas, pray for us.